C000244702

THE ART OF THE

THEATRE WORKSHOP

COMPILED AND INTRODUCED
BY MURRAY MELVIN

OBERON BOOKS
LONDON

First published in 2006 by Oberon Books Ltd

521 Caledonian Road, London N7 9RH

Tel: 020 7607 3637 / Fax: 020 7607 3629

e-mail: info@oberonbooks.com

www.oberonbooks.com

Text copyright © Murray Melvin 2006

Collection copyright © Theatre Royal Stratford East 2006

Photographs and images copyright © the copyright holders

Murray Melvin is hereby identified as author of this text, and Theatre Royal Stratford East as compiler of this collection, in accordance with section 77 of the Copyright, Designs and Patents Act 1988. The author and compiler have asserted their moral rights.

This book is sold subject to the condition that it shall not by way of trade or otherwise be circulated without the publisher's consent in any form of binding or cover or circulated electronically other than that in which it is published and without a similar condition including this condition being imposed on any subsequent purchaser.

A catalogue record for this book is available from the British Library.

Front cover: *The Other Animals* by Ewan MacColl, photograph by John Spinner, set design by John Bury. Inside front: *Oh What a Lovely War*, photograph by Romano Cagnoni, costumes designed by Una Collins. Inside back: *Arden of Faversham*, photograph by John Spinner, set design by John Bury.

Book and cover design: Dan Steward

ISBN: 1 84002 691 X / 978-1-84002-691-7

Printed in Great Britain by CPI Bath

With love and gratitude for my university

Gerry Raffles   Joan Littlewood   John Bury

Theatre Royal Stratford East in supported by:

Thanks to the supporters of the Theatre Royal.

We thank the major supporters of Theatre Royal Stratford East for their continuing support: Arts Council England, London Borough of Newham, London Councils and Channel 4 to support our work to develop new musicals.

We would also like to thank the Funders and Supporters of Theatre Royal Stratford East: The Big Lottery Fund, Connecting Communities Plus (DCLG), Esmée Fairbairn Foundation, European Social Fund, Football Foundation, Garfield Weston Foundation, Grange Park Opera, Harold Hyam Wingate Foundation, Heritage Lottery Fund, Jack Petchey Foundation, King Baudouin Foundation, Mercers' Company, Money Gram, PRS Foundation.

www.stratfordeast.com

CONTENTS

ACKNOWLEDGEMENTS

My sincere thanks to:

Kerry Michael, Artistic Director, Theatre Royal Stratford East, for listening to my thoughts about this book and making them happen;

James Hogan, Publisher, Oberon Books, who was attracted by the idea and has given me every encouragement and guidance to bring the project to fruition;

Imelda Spinner – her lovely John's negatives were the inspiration for this book;

Howard Goorney, for permission to use extracts from his book *The Theatre Workshop Story*;

Jean (MacColl) Newlove, for allowing me to use quotes from the Ewan MacColl articles in the *Theatre Quarterly*;

Howard (Harry) Greene, Joan's first designer, for permission to use his illustrations. And for his remembrance of things past;

Harriet & Red Mason and Jessica & Robin Sutcliffe, for donating the artwork of Ernest Brooks and Barbara Niven to the Theatre Royal Archive;

George Mayhew, in remembrance of his graphics for the programmes;

Sophie Wolchover, for allowing me to reproduce the costume designs by her mother Una Collins for *Oh What a Lovely War*;

Romano Cagnoni, for the photographs of *Oh What a Lovely War*;

The Staff of the Theatre Royal Stratford East – they have all shown such patience and helpfulness during the gestation period of the book, especially Silvia Pilotto, Stuart Saunders and Mary Ling. I am most grateful;

The Staff of Oberon Books for their enthusiasm and expertise;

John Munday for all things photographic;

Andrew Baker for allowing me to reproduce his photograph from the National Portrait Gallery;

And my admiration to the founding members of both Theatre Union and Theatre Workshop who by dint of dedication, hard work, inspiration and imagination created a unique Workshop of the Theatre.

Murray Melvin

Theatre Royal, August 2006

TEXTUAL SOURCES AND FURTHER READING

Howard Goorney, *The Theatre Workshop Story* (London, Eyre Methuen, 1981),
  extracts reproduced with permission of A & C Black Publishers

Nadine Holdsworth, *Joan Littlewood* (London, Routledge, 2006)

Robert Leach, *Theatre Workshop* (Exeter, University of Exeter Press, 2006)

Joan Littlewood's *Peculiar History As She Tells It* (London, Methuen, 1994)

Ewan MacColl, 'Grass Roots of the Theatre Workshop', *Theatre Quarterly*
  Volume III, Number 9 (January–March 1973), pp 58–68

Jean Newlove, *Laban for Actors and Dancers* (London, Nick Hern Books, 1993)

IMAGES

All material in the book is taken from the Theatre Royal Stratford East Archive:

Lantern slide designs by Ernest Brooks: pp 28, 29

Photographs by Romano Cagnoni: pp 109, 111, 112, 114–19, 121, 122

Costume designs by Una Collins: pp 109, 110, 113, 120

Photograph by David Sim: p 121 (© Guardian News & Media Ltd 1963)

Photographs by John Spinner: pp 41–61, 63–9, 71–84, 86, 87, 89–93, 99, 100, 102, 103.

Every effort has been made to trace and contact the owners of the copyright for all images reproduced in the book. Acknowledgement has been made in all instances where the copyright owner is known.

A NOTE ON THE TEXT

This publication is a celebration of the *art* of the Theatre Workshop, and I have focused on this aspect of the Workshop's history. The *story* of the company has been told in greater detail elsewhere, and those in search of more background information should consider the books listed opposite.

MM

The name 'Theatre Workshop' is synonymous with Joan Littlewood's landmark productions of the 1950s and 60s: *The Quare Fellow* and *The Hostage* by Brendan Behan; *A Taste of Honey* by Shelagh Delaney; *Fings Ain't Wot They Used T'Be* by Frank Norman and Lionel Bart; and the company's First World War musical *Oh What a Lovely War*. Even those too young to have seen them will know their names because they are part of theatrical folklore.

These productions originated at the Theatre Royal Stratford-atte-Bow in London's East End, home of the Theatre Workshop Company, and transferred to the West End and beyond to great critical acclaim. Now exalted as glittering successes of post-war London and a colourful chapter in British theatre history, they were in fact the culmination of a grittier story that started in Manchester during the depression years.

THE RED MEGAPHONES: SALFORD

The agit-prop group The Red Megaphones was founded in 1930. Its name was taken from the most famous German such group of the time, the 'Rote Sprachrohr'. Agit-prop – 'agitation' and 'propaganda' – was to become an international movement, which bound groups all over the world in a common purpose, to dramatise social and political issues of the time.

The peak of the Red Megaphones' street activity and political involvement was during the Lancashire textile strikes of 1932. A driving force in that early Manchester group was a young James H Miller, who was later to transform himself into the folk singer Ewan MacColl.

A phrase used by agit-prop groups of the time was:

A PROPERTYLESS THEATRE FOR
THE PROPERTYLESS CLASS

James H Miller, aka Ewan MacColl

In 1973 MacColl wrote an article entitled 'Grass Roots of the Theatre Workshop' for the *Theatre Quarterly* in which he looked back on this difficult but important time. In it he states:

> Mining and Textiles were the basic industries in the city [Salford], and these were hard hit by the economic crisis [...] In any working-class street, one third of the men [...] were unemployed, and three-quarters of their families were affected by unemployment through the means test. [...] If you knew a lot about this, and you were going to write sketches about it, the form would to some extent reflect [...] one's own grievances and bitterness. And almost without knowing we stumbled upon a form which wasn't really so different from that of the old mumming plays – the *Seven Champions of Christendom*, say. It was merely that the heroes and the villains had taken on twentieth century garb. (p 58)

The means test was a humiliating investigation by the local authorities into personal and family income and possessions before any relief was sanctioned.

Howard Goorney was also a member of the Workshop Company from the early days in Manchester. In his book *The Theatre Workshop Story* he recalls:

> The Group performed short sketches against the hated Means Test to dole queues outside Labour Exchanges, sometimes to sixty or seventy people. To keep pace with an ever changing situation, they developed a form of instant theatre; sketches written in the morning were performed to the afternoon dole queues. [...] To an audience that was on the dole, no subtlety was required. [...] Though the Group were in their early teens and lacking in theatrical experience and skills [...] the essence of street theatre lay in its simplicity and directness. The actors who represented types rather than individual characters were of the same class and background as the audience, so there was no gap between them. [...] The three actors in 'Rent, Interest and Profit' all wore identical clothes – bib and brace overalls and top hats with 'R' 'I' and 'P' on them. (p 2)

Sketch from 1962 by Harry H Greene, based on a photograph of the 'Red Megaphones' performing on the streets of Manchester in 1932

POLITICS, IN ITS FULLEST SENSE,
MEANS THE AFFAIRS OF THE PEOPLE.
IN THIS SENSE THE PLAYS DONE
WILL BE POLITICAL.

– Theatre of Action manifesto

Howard Goorney also recalls that:

> By the end of 1933 [...] with the rise of Hitler to power in
> Germany, and the spread of International Fascism [...] the
> Group felt that the broader political issues that now had to be
> faced could not be encompassed within the limitations of street
> theatre. [...] From the purely practical point of view, most people
> were not prepared to stand in the cold for any length of time.
> [...] Also, as it got dark in the evenings around 3.30 in the North
> of England, it was only possible to play during the day, which
> meant limiting the audience to the unemployed. (p 5)

THE MOVE INDOORS, 1934

It was during this vibrant period that Joan Littlewood arrived in Manchester. The BBC's Northern Region had at this time the most remarkable radio features, using montage material with music, song and a narrator. The device of the narrator combined field reporting with story-telling. Joan was working for the British Broadcasting Corporation on one such radio programme about the Mersey Tunnel, and Ewan MacColl was also working for the radio department as an actor. When their paths crossed they quickly found they had similar ideas – about a kind of theatre far removed from the usual fare served up to the public of the time.

The English theatrical establishment had always protected itself from European influences; productions were incredibly static, with polite arguments, monologues or duologues, and a lack of imperative action on stage. Joan and Ewan's enthusiasm, however, extended across many European movements, among them Vsevolod Meyerhold's system of bio-mechanics and Erwin Piscator's insistence on training his actors as dancers in the schools of Rudolf von Laban. It was no coincidence that they named the next group 'Theatre of Action'.

This meeting between MacColl and Littlewood was a turning point. Out of their collaboration the agit-prop group of mainly amateur performers made their first moves towards becoming a professional company. The group evolved as Joan's concepts of theatre evolved: so came the need to stage more substantial works, accompanied by light and sound.

One group member, Victor (Alf) Armitt, set out on a quest for knowledge about theatrical lighting – a completely new subject for this untrained company. Browsing the shelves of his local library, he discovered the theories of Adolphe Appia, the Swiss scenic designer, in *The Nature and Function of Stage Lighting*. With the aid of a pocket dictionary he read Appia's famous treatise; literally translating every word, Alf mastered the theory and then built himself a switchboard to put the theory into practice. With this unorthodox education he became the group's lighting expert.

Ewan MacColl remembers: 'He'd never read anything about the use of light in the theatre except Appia – he hadn't come across Meyerhold's theories about exposing the works, he wasn't genned up on the work of people like Piscator [...], but he hit upon it all himself [...] and it was largely as a result of his feeling for light that we used light like we did [...] I believe any bad work we ever did in lighting was in direct contradiction to what he would have taught.' ('Grass Roots', p 60)

As Howard Goorney reminds us, 'Appia believed in a comprehensive artistic unity on the stage; a bringing together of dance, music, lighting and painting, a synthesis of all the arts.' Instead of using lights merely to illuminate painted sets, Appia's theory would 'combine with the three dimensional or architectural type of setting, and actually arouse an emotional response in the audience.' These theories came as 'an exciting revelation, resolving and clarifying [...] the whole relationship of an actor to the space in which he works, and to music, light and all the elements which went to make up the flexible theatre they were seeking.' (*Theatre Workshop Story*, p 5)

The company put these theories into full practice in their 1947 production of Ewan MacColl's adaptation of Aristophanes' *Lysistrata*, called *Operation Olive Branch*.

Operation Olive Branch, 1947
Edward Horton and Howard Goorney

The revelation of Appia's theories was followed by the discovery of Leon Moussinac's book *The New Movement in Theatre*, published in English in 1931, which brought together the major European theatre practices of the time. To the young members of the group, raised on a British theatre insulated from theatrical movements on the continent, these theories seemed revolutionary, and would influence the whole approach of the company's future work.

The Peace Ballot in 1935 demonstrated the support of the British people for collective security through the League of Nations and against re-armament. It secured millions of votes and the Tory Government, led by Stanley Baldwin, came to power on the basis of support for this policy.

It was against this background that in 1936 Joan Littlewood and Ewan MacColl were asked by The Peace Pledge Union to mount a production of the anti-war play *Miracle at Verdun* by Hans Chlumberg. A cast of nearly 150 was required for the production, but with help from The Peace Pledge Union and the Quaker Movement contact was made with amateur groups over a wide area of Lancashire. Universities supplied students for the foreign nationalities, and the Friends Meeting House was put at the company's disposal for rehearsals.

The play was performed for two weeks at Manchester's Lesser Free Trade Hall and was a tremendous success. Out of the enthusiasm of this production emerged enough people with time, energy and commitment to form a permanent group that took the name:

THEATRE UNION

The new group issued a manifesto.

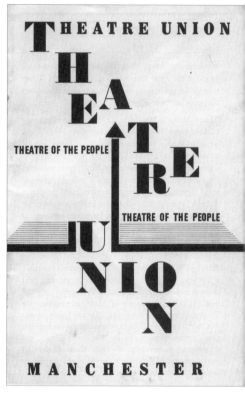

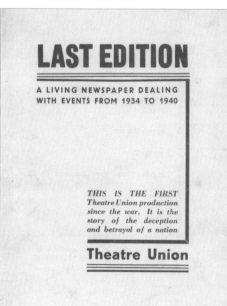

manifesto

THE THEATRE must face up to the problems of its time; it cannot ignore the poverty and human suffering which increases every day. It cannot, with sincerity, close its eyes to the disasters of its time. Means Test suicides, wars, fascism and the million sordid accidents reported in the daily press. If the theatre of to-day would reach the heights achieved four thousand years ago in Greece and four hundred years ago in Elizabethan England it must face up to such problems. To those who say that such affairs are not the concern of the theatre or that the theatre should confine itself to treading in the paths of ' beauty ' and ' dignity ', we would say " Read Shakespeare, Marlowe, Webster, Sophocles, Aeschylus, Aristophanes, Calderon, Moliere, Lope-de-Vega, Schiller and the rest." The Theatre Union says that in facing up to the problems of our time and by intensifying our efforts to get at the essence of reality, we are also attempting to solve our own theatrical problems both technical and ideological. By doing this we are ensuring the future of the theatre, a future which will not be born in the genteel atmosphere of retirement and seclusion, but rather in the clash and turmoil of the battles between the oppressors and the oppressed.

theatre union

THE THEATRE OF THE PEOPLE

I enclose P.O. value .... as I wish to become a member of Theatre Union at 6d. per annum, Unemployed Worker: 3d. per annum, Member of Affiliated Organisation, 3d. per annum (Please state organisation).

NAME, ADDRESS AND DATE:

✳ Please use Block Letters and State whether Mr., Mrs. or Miss. Further Membership Application forms obtainable from
THE SECRETARY, THEATRE UNION, 111 GROSVENOR ST., M/cr. 1

ELECTRIC [C] PRINTING CO LTD. [T.U.] MANCHESTER. 8.

Theatre Union and its work ethos began to attract attention and drew into the company artists and craftsmen with particular skills. They included Barbara Niven, a lecturer at Manchester Art College, and Ernest Brooks, artist and illustrator, who were to become responsible for the design element. The painter L S Lowry also offered his help.

THE SPANISH CIVIL WAR, 1936

It was decided to mount the first production in England of Lope de Vega's early seventeenth-century Spanish classic *Fuente Ovejuna*. The story of the uprising of the villagers of Fuente Ovejuna against the tyranny of their feudal overlords mirrored in many ways the struggle of the Spanish people against Fascism at the time. Adapted by Ewan MacColl and translated as *The Sheepwell*, the production was not just about entertainment: its purpose was to help with fund-raising for the food ship that the city of Manchester was sending to Spain.

The décor group started on the project. They designed and built a set consisting of an abstract backcloth of all the colours associated with Spain, together with a water well and a beautiful large sculpted sheep.

CAST

The Commander Fernan Gomez	MARTIN GOULD
Laurencia	JOAN LITTLEWOOD
Flores	CYRIL HALLIGAN
Ortuno	SYDNEY ISAAC
Cimbranas	GERARD DAVIES
Esteban	GERALD BUCKLEY
Juan Rojo	ROBERT MCLEISH
Alonso	... HENRY SUSS
Cuadrado	VICTOR A. ARMITT
Frondoso	KENNETH CASE
Mengo	... JOE DRUCK
Barrildo	R. SCOTT HANDLEY
Leonelo	WILLIAM BELCHER
Pascuola	LYDIA M. RITCHIE
Jacinta	MOYA STEVENS
Musicians	LAIDLEY BROS.
Peasants	BILL SHARPLES, ROSE BABSLEY, AILEEN BELCHER, JOHN CHEETHAM, JACQUELINE COLBERT
Dancer	AUDREY LLOYD

• • • • •

DANCE INTERLUDES conceived by Audrey Lloyd
DECOR by Barbara Niven, Bill Sharples, Ern Brooks
COSTUMES designed by Barbara Niven, Ern Brooks
executed by Madeline Lockwood

STAGE MANAGER	George K. Hall, A.I.L. (sp.)
LIGHTING	... Kenneth Hartley
STAGE CARPENTER	Ernest Large
PRODUCTION SECRETARY	Moya Stephens
ORGANISER	Joan Whittenbury
BUSINESS MANAGER	N. Harold Lever

Page Four

ACT I

Dance Interlude. " The Ruled."

Scene I. The Square in Fuente Ove Juna.
Scene II. A field outside the village.

•

ACT II

Dance Interlude. " The Rulers."

Scene I. The Square in Fuente Ove Juna.
Scene II. A field outside the village.
Scene III. A room in Juan Rojo's house.
Scene IV. The Square in Fuente Ove Juna.

•

INTERVAL 20 MINUTES

•

ACT III

Dance Interlude. " The Killing."

Scene I. Outside the Town Hall in Fuente Ove Juna.
Scene II. A Hall in the Commander's Castle.
Scene III. The Square in Fuente Ove Juna.
Scene IV. Outside the Town Hall in Fuente Ove Juna.

Page Five

THEATRE UNION ● FOOD FOR SPAIN ● THEATRE UNION

FUENTE OVEJUNA

LOPE DE VEGA

FOOD FOR SPAIN ● THEATRE UNION ● FOOD FOR SPAIN

The Sheepwell (Fuente Ovejuna) by Lope de Vega,
Adapted by Ewan MacColl, 1936

Ewan MacColl recalled with fondness this set: 'I think we had more affection for that sculpted sheep than anything that had happened right through the whole period of the development of our theatre – it was tangible, something you could see and touch. And you could stand on the rim of the well, besides.' ('Grass Roots', p 65)

THE GOOD SOLDIER SCHWEIK: MANCHESTER, 1939

Erwin Piscator had adapted and staged Jaroslav Hašek's *The Good Soldier Schweik* in Berlin in 1928. Eleven years later, as the threat of a second world war loomed, the Theatre Union staged a translation of Piscator's version at the Lesser Free Trade Hall. The company lacked the technical forces available to Piscator, such as his moving platforms and escalators, but they did maintain his mix of living actors and cartoon figures, which was a major stylistic leap at the time. And, for the first time in Britain, they used the innovation of back-lit projection.

Such advances involved the exertion of many creative minds, as Ewan MacColl points out: 'The Germans were the only people who had the right back-projecting equipment, so we got a group of young technicians and inventors from Metropolitan Vickers in Manchester actually to invent machines that could project these things, and they were marvellous.' ('Grass Roots', p 63)

The designs for Schweik's journey were created by Ernest Brooks, drawn out onto large sheets of paper and then transferred onto small glass slides for use in the projector.

Ernest Brooks' line drawings used in the ground-breaking
back-lit projections of *The Good Soldier Schweik*, 1939

THE SECOND WORLD WAR, 1939–45

Right from the start of the war the company was planning its post-war future. The members of the group promised to stay in touch, in the hope that they might one day work together again. They vowed to use the time to develop the theoretical work of the company by finding out about the great theatres of the past. Each of them would become a specialist in a chosen aspect of theatre, or study in depth the traditions of a particular movement or style, and they would somehow share their knowledge, wherever the war might send them. A series of letters crossed the globe, as this group of friends continued to communicate in spite of their separation.

Not all of them survived. Graham Banks, a company member who had acquired a profound knowledge of Greek Theatre, was killed in a bombing raid over Hamburg. Bill Sharples, a gifted sculptor and scenic designer, was deep in his studies of stage design when blown up by a land-mine in an oil tanker. A nucleus of the old Theatre Union came through, but they sadly and sorely missed their absent friends. The company has always been a close-knit family, and a pain for one is a pain for all.

After demobilisation the survivors came together again in Manchester. Collectively they now knew more about the history of world theatre than probably any other group of players in the country. They pooled their gratuities and started to buy electrical equipment and the basic necessities to start a company.

In Joan Littlewood's *Peculiar History As She Tells It*, also known as *Joan's Book*, she recalls a meeting of this newly formed group:

'What are we calling our theatre?' asked Howard [Goorney]. 'When it's christened it's born.'

'Well, we've had Action and Union.'

Someone hit the right note. I wrote it across my diary: 'The Workshop'. A Theatre, a workshop? Everybody made fun of it, but years after, 'Workshops' sprang up all over the place. Everything was a Workshop, from two councillors meeting in the pub to a baby show. (p 158)

theatre workshop

MANIFESTO

- The great theatres of all times have been popular theatres, theatres which reflected the dreams and struggles of the people of their time. The theatre of Aeschylus and Sophocles, of Shakespeare and Ben Jonson, of the Commedia del Arte and Moliere derived their inspiration, their language, their art from the common people.

- Today in Britain, there is no popular theatre ; there has been no popular theatre since the Jacobean age. Only a very small percentage of the population of Great Britain has ever been inside a theatre, this in spite of the fact that great numbers of people are organised as never before, into political organisations, social bodies, and trade unions.

- The theatre of twentieth century Britain is the property of a very small section of society ; its dramaturgy generally reflects the life of this small group, a life so trivial that it is without interest for the really important sections of society, the miners, engineers, weavers, dockers, and all those who are involved in building a new world.

- The great events of our time, wars, social upheavals, the frustration of man's social desires, and the attempts to build a new civilisation find little expression in the contemporary theatre.

- We in *theatre workshop* want to remedy this.

- We want a theatre which will speak for the common people, a theatre which will restore the great plays of the past to their rightful place—that is with the people.

- We want a theatre with a living language, a theatre which is not afraid of the sound of its own voice and which will comment as fearlessly on society as Ben Jonson and Aristophanes did.

- *theatre workshop* is a team of skilled artists and technicians who have broken with the moribund conventions of the commercial theatre. We believe that by combining all that is best in the great theatres of the past with the most recent scientific and technical developments we can create a theatrical form sufficiently flexible to reflect the rapidly changing twentieth century scene.

- The theatre must become a great art again and this cannot happen unless it becomes an important part of the life of the working people.

PUBLISHED BY "theatre workshop," 112 HIGHGATE, KENDAL, WESTMORLAND

THEATRE WORKSHOP

So a new voyage of discovery began with an intense training programme at its core. The audience required a sense of timing and speed from the performers, corresponding to the changes of the period. The company had to keep up with the pace of modern society. Joan Littlewood was well aware that the acting of the day was slow and static. Even in the early days she had introduced movement into the company's work.

The sources were both American and German but the destiny of Theatre Workshop was more closely linked to that of Germany because of the direct influence of Rudolf von Laban, who had migrated to England in 1938. He founded his own school in Manchester in 1946. Jean Newlove had been an assistant to Laban, and she joined the Workshop and became their movement teacher and choreographer. She explained how popular audiences, accustomed to the experience of watching movies, came to expect an equivalent level of invention, intensity and movement from their theatrical entertainments. In her book *Laban for Actors and Dancers*, she quotes from a newspaper review of the triumphant Swedish tour of 1968, which ended at a packed Royal Opera House in Stockholm:

> …a company of actors who can use movement to describe gun-fights, storms, the sea, the tension between people… The speed and suppleness of the actors comes not only from well-trained bodies. It is the result of a dynamic technique of movement. This is the system of Rudolf Laban. (pp 8–9)

Although the company received critical praise over the following years, the battle against poverty and for recognition of their work was a constant struggle. Intermittent homelessness was just one consequence of their financial situation: with no public subsidy, no funding and no permanent performing space, it was a hand-to-mouth existence.

Touring was the order of the day. From mining villages to local school halls, the Theatre Workshop appeared at venues from Wales to Scotland and across the north of England. These were mainly one-night stands or short bookings in out-of-season theatres with long journeys in between.

Surviving in short-term digs, living communally on minimal wages or sometimes no wages at all, their base was a building on the Oxford Road in Manchester and their transport a rather old lorry. But amid material hardship it was a time of intense commitment, collaboration and creativity.

As one of the first companies to establish experimental theatre at Edinburgh, they appeared in 1946 at the Little Theatre, then again in 1949 at Epworth Hall. (By 1951 at the Oddfellows Hall and again the following year with their production of Ewan MacColl's *The Travellers*, they made the fringe events as important as the main festival. It was not until 1962 at The Traverse that the Fringe became 'official'.) But still the funding bodies in their own country ignored them.

Gerry Raffles had joined the company aged just sixteen and by now had taken on the role of company manager. During the Christmas season of 1949–50, Gerry was seeking dates to fill the winter schedule. They were presenting *Alice in Wonderland*, and a call to a Theatre Royal at Stratford, in the East End of London, resulted in an offer for the first week of January. So, by happen-chance, the Workshop lorry, with set, costumes and members of the company, travelled south.

By 1952, after years of touring (still on the lorry; still mostly one- or two-night appearances) and in ongoing poverty, the company were yet to find a permanent home. They had played the Edinburgh Festival that year and were now surviving in Glasgow. The need for a building of their own where they could rehearse and play became a priority. The sheer physical effort and long working hours involved in one-night fit-ups were beginning to take their toll.

At one of the regular company meetings held during their stay in Glasgow, Gerry Raffles announced that the Theatre Royal in London, where they had played some two and a half years earlier, was now closed but was available to rent. After a great deal of discussion they took what was to prove the most momentous decision in the history of Theatre Workshop: to lease the Theatre Royal Stratford for a trial period. A majority of the company felt they had endured the strain of touring for too long. They acquired a lease for an initial six weeks. It was six weeks that have never ended.

THEATRE ROYAL STRATFORD-ATTE-BOW, 1953

Harry Greene recalls his arrival in Stratford:

> It was dark [...] The theatre was situated in a back street amongst back-to-back terraced houses, a street market smelling, after the day's trading, of over-ripe discarded fruit, rotting vegetables and paraffin lamps. [...] The theatre inside was damp-smelling and dismal, the drains were foul, there was the staleness of old clothes, old make-up and lack of ventilation. Plans went ahead so quickly there wasn't time to stop and think. I was ordering posters, booking advertising space, designing front-of-house publicity posters and pictures, organising local labour to clean up the dressing-rooms ready for the arrival of the Company. Gerry dealt with administration, newspapers, box-office, catering, local authorities, all essential to the setting up of a repertory theatre. For that was what we were to become. (*Theatre Workshop Story*, p 90)

Another member, actor George A Cooper, continues:

> I remember walking into this rather broken-down theatre. We just couldn't afford digs, so we had to sleep in the dressing rooms, which is against the rules. [...] I had quite a nice time in my little dressing room. I devised all sorts of gastronomic marvels, like apple omelettes for breakfast. (*Theatre Workshop Story*, p 90)

Sketch by Harry H Greene of the Theatre Royal, Stratford, upon arrival in 1953.
Below the sketch he has written: 'After years of touring & enjoying the country
air in Scotland, North East Coast & Wales, we find ourselves living & working in
the acrid, sulphur-laden, heavily polluted air of London's East End.'

The actor Harry H Corbett, who later became famous as Harold Steptoe in *Steptoe and Son*, also had vivid memories:

> Taking your turn to go down into the cellars and get that terrible anthracite boiler going. You never had enough coal and you could only burn it when the audience came in.' (*Theatre Workshop Story,* p 90)

Howard Goorney writes that the traders and shopkeepers of Angel Lane (running down one side of the theatre) took the players to their hearts, 'particularly Bert and May at the Café L'Ange, where extra large helpings and credit were always available'. (p91) Such generosity made easier the lives of the company members who were working incredibly long hours: not only rehearsing and promoting the show, they were also busy cleaning and maintaining the building itself.

On my own arrival as a student in 1957 the Café L'Ange was still a haven for the hungry and weary members of the Workshop. The heavy physical days, both on and off stage, meant that we were continually ravenous. A plate of Bert and May's home-cooked ham with English mustard, though not affordable on a daily basis, was a treat when funds permitted.

Working in an unheated theatre without hot food also added to the hunger pains. In the cold winter months we would often break a rehearsal to take a movement class in order to defrost our brains and bodies. As mentioned by Harry Corbett, the boiler in the basement was only lit one hour before the start of the performance – and then only to heat the auditorium. When the curtain was raised the wave of cold air from the stage would hit the stalls. The unfortunate actor who started the play knew his or her opening moments would be lost whilst the audience recovered from the blast.

Despite all the hardships the company opened at the Theatre Royal, Stratford-atte-Bow on 2 February 1953, with Shakespeare's *Twelfth Night*. The programme for this first production boldly states their intention:

A SEASON OF GREAT PLAYS

In the audience for that opening production was a young man who was soon to become an important figure for the art of the Theatre Workshop. His name was John Spinner.

The Spinners were a Walthamstow family. John's father was an amateur photographer and John followed in his footsteps. John became an Electronics Engineer and later a Medical Researcher at St Bartholomew's Medical College. Hearing about an innovative theatre company who had taken over the nearby Theatre Royal, he took himself across to Stratford. He was so excited by the performance that afterwards he approached Gerry Raffles and offered to take the company's production photographs.

The Workshop had no money for the luxury of a photographer. Nevertheless John agreed to do the work on a voluntary basis out of his admiration for the company. He became part of the Workshop family and continued taking their photographs until the early 1970s.

When in 1993 Philip Hedley, Artistic Director of the Theatre Royal at the time, asked me to take on the task of organising an archive of the Theatre Workshop Company, I remembered the wonderful photographs John had taken. I contacted him and was invited to tea at his home with his wife Imelda.

Having ascertained that he still had all his original negatives of the Workshop images, I asked him to pick two of his favourite shots from each production and print them for inclusion in the archive.

Being, I now realise, an archivist in the making, I also enquired if he had any plans for the final destination of all these negatives? He looked across to his wife and said, 'Isn't that a coincidence?' Imelda concurred. 'Murray,' he explained, 'only last week I said to Imelda, What will become of this collection when I am gone?'

I quickly suggested he might like the idea of them 'coming home'. On the promise that they would be well looked after, perhaps he would consider donating them all to the Theatre Royal? He was overjoyed at this suggestion:

'Murray, I cannot think of anything I would like more.'

'That's settled then. When I return to the theatre I shall write a letter to the board stating that at some date in the future when the negatives come into our possession, they will be taken into the theatre's archive and known as "The John Spinner Collection".'

I left full of excitement, taking with me a couple of old programmes for the archive which John had kept.

Alas, within a few months of that joyous tea party I had a call from Imelda telling me that her lovely John had had a massive heart attack and was gone. 'All his negatives are here,' she told me, 'but in rather a muddle because he was in the process of sorting them all out for you. However, I know how pleased he was at the thought that they would end up in the theatre's archive, so of course, they are all yours.'

It was a sad task going through the negatives and putting them all in order, but I have kept my promise. They form the foundation of the archive for that period in the theatre's history, and one photograph from every production he shot is displayed on the walls of the Theatre Workshop Bar with a commemorative plaque, 'The John Spinner Collection'. It is my fervent hope that he would approve of my selection.

The following pages feature John Spinner's photographs from the productions of the years 1953 to 1960 at Stratford East.

1953

INTRODUCTION TO THE SEASON

Theatre Workshop is a company which survives critics and crises by having the courage of its convictions. Among these is the belief that the art of theatre is still capable of development; that this art can and will be a necessary part of people's lives; that theatre should be grand, vulgar, simple, pathetic… but not genteel, not poetical.

We have tested our theories, ventured the boards with all the music-hall turns of 'the new movements in the theatre' and when they failed us we've had to pass the hat round or take to honest labour, for our critics and supporters were miners, cottonworkers and steelworkers who haven't much time for mere artistic experiment.

But we survived! We learned how to make our experiments work! We have known success – an evening in a Welsh miners' hall, perhaps, when the show was good, when we shared with our audience a great imaginative experience – times, here and there, which have been worth all the years of work.

Joan Littlewood

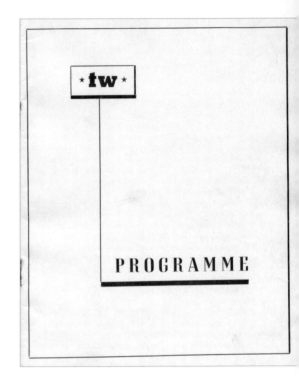

The credo of the Theatre Workshop was to present the best of European and Contemporary Drama. In their first season in 1953, having arrived at a broken-down Theatre Royal, their programming is a testament to those ideals.

Paradise Street by Ewan MacColl, 1953

Juno and the Paycock by Sean O'Casey, 1953

Colour Guard by George Styles, 1953

Arms and the Man by George Bernard Shaw, 1953

Lysistrata by Aristophanes,
Adapted by Ewan MacColl, 1953

Three Men on a Horse by George Abbott, Translated by Theatre Workshop, 1953

Anna Christie by Eugene O'Neill, 1953

Uncle Vanya by Anton Chekhov, 1953

The Alchemist by Ben Jonson, 1953

The Government Inspector by Nikolai Gogol, Translated by John Evans, 1953

A Christmas Carol by Charles Dickens, Adapted by Joan Littlewood, 1953

Treasure Island by Robert Louis Stevenson, Adapted by Joan Littlewood, 1953
A stockade was needed, six feet high. Harry Greene and Karl Woods set off for
Epping Forest. At midnight, out of the blue, sirens screeching, batons drawn:
the boys in blue. Harry and Karl were taken to West Ham Police Station and
detained; rescued by Gerry Raffles at seven the next morning. However, the
sympathetic sergeant had seen a play at the Royal, so he and his squad got free
tickets and the theatre got its stockade. The police also donated castor wheels
from old laundry baskets to help with the set.

1954

Richard II by William Shakespeare, 1954

This production coincided with that of the Old Vic Theatre in which Richard was played by John Neville. The Workshop Richard was Harry H Corbett, who later found fame in the *Steptoe* series. Comparisons were drawn by the critics of course, and it brought a recognition among the wider public that Stratford East did exist. Those of us lucky enough to have seen the Stratford production will recall the lack of elongated fanfares, long gold cloaks and even longer processionals. But etched in one's memory are the filmic overlapping of scenes and raw Elizabethan language. Poetry spoken on the moment not on the breath.

Van Call by Anthony Nicholson, 1954
A play commissioned from a local journalist, set in contemporary
Stratford. It is a policy on local subjects continued to the present day.

The Dutch Courtesan by John Marston, 1954
First production for 300 years. It has a line in the prologue that Marston could have
written for the Theatre Workshop credo: 'Best art presents not what it can but should.'

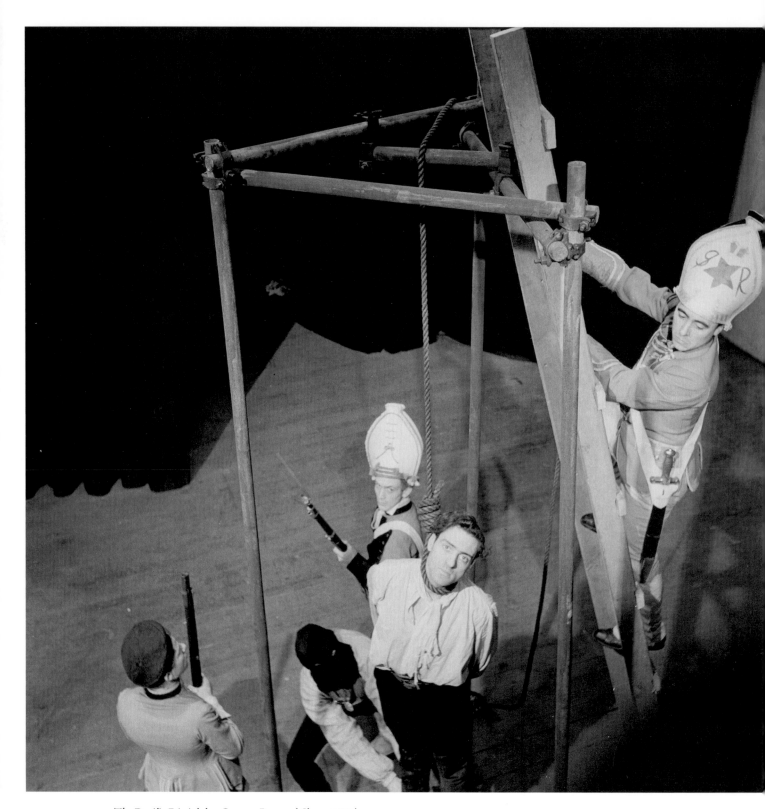

The Devil's Disciple by George Bernard Shaw, 1954

The Fire Eaters by Charles Fenn, 1954

Red Roses For Me by Sean O'Casey, 1954
A tree was needed for the set designed by John Bury. A real one.
Harry Greene set off again, with help, for Epping Forest. The
requirement was a tree with a twelve-foot span. They found it.
This time without intervention from any local authority.

Jupiter's Night Out, Based on *Amphytrion 38* by Jean Giraudoux, 1954

An Enemy of the People by Henrik Ibsen, Adaptation by Theatre Workshop, 1954

Long Voyage Home by Eugene O'Neill, 1954

THEATRE ROYAL

STRATFORD   **E. 15**

MARYLAND 5973: 6/- 4/6 3/6 2/6 1/6
TUES – FRI 7.45   SAT 5.30 & 8.30
TUBE STRATFORD: BUSES STR. B'WY

THEATRE WORKSHOP

PRIOR TO PRESENTATION AT THE
PARIS INTERNATIONAL FESTIVAL

ARDEN OF FAVERSHAM

AN UNUSUAL AND EXCITING THRILLER
PRODUCED BY JOAN LITTLEWOOD

Arden of Faversham, Author unknown, 1954
Another classic from the English canon rescued by the company and,
as with *The Dutch Courtesan*, the first production for over 300 years.

The Good Soldier Schweik by Jaroslav Hašek, Adapted by Ewan MacColl, 1954

The Chimes by Charles Dickens, Adapted by Joan Littlewood, 1954

The Prince and the Pauper by Mark Twain, Adapted by Ewan MacColl, 1954

1955

The Other Animals by Ewan MacColl, 1955

Volpone by Ben Jonson, 1955
A modern dress production that was not cut or changed from the original
script. Relocated to present-day Italy as a satire on spivs and hangers-on, this,
together with *Arden of Faversham*, took the Paris International Festival by storm.

GLADIATORS
ONLY

Androcles and the Lion by George Bernard Shaw, 1955

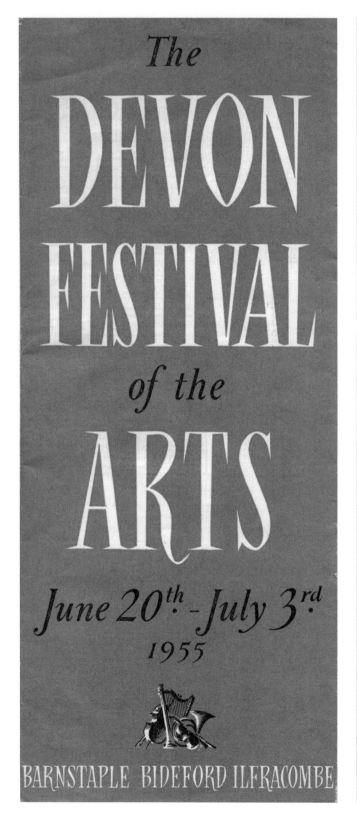

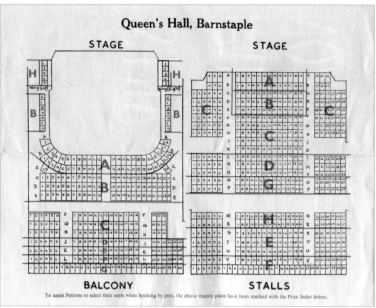

Queen's Hall, Barnstaple

STAGE   STAGE

BALCONY   STALLS

To assist Patrons to select their seats when booking by post, the above theatre plans have been marked with the Price Index letters.

THE QUEEN'S HALL, BARNSTAPLE
Saturday, 25th June, 7.30 p.m. to 11.30 p.m.
THE KEN MOULE SEVEN
Tickets (Limited) : 5/6

DRAMA
THE QUEEN'S HALL, BARNSTAPLE
Monday, 27th June, and Week

OSCAR LEWENSTEIN *presents*
The THEATRE WORKSHOP COMPANY

Monday, Tuesday and Wednesday, at 7.30 p.m.
Matinee : Wednesday at 2.15 p.m.
RICHARD II
By William Shakespeare.

Thursday, Friday and Saturday at 7.30 p.m.
Matinee : Saturday at 2.15 p.m.
The first English presentation of
MOTHER COURAGE
By Bertolt Brecht, translated by Eric Bentley.
Music by Dessau.
The Plays Produced by Joan Littlewood.

Seats bookable :
(A & B) 8/6, (C) 7/-, (D & E) 5/6, (F) 4/-. Unreserved :
(G & H) 2/6.

CHAMBER CONCERTS
THE PALACE THEATRE, BIDEFORD
Tuesday, 28th June, at 7.30 p.m.
The
LONDON HARPSICHORD ENSEMBLE

Trio in C for flute, violin and continuo............de Fesch
Suite for viola de gamba and harpsichord
                         de Caix D'Hervelois
Sonata in A for harpsichord and flute...............*Bach*
The Apotheosis of Corelli, for flute, violin and continuo
                              Couperin
Sonata in A for violin and harpsichord..............*Handel*
The Italian Concerto for harpsichord solo...........*Bach*
Trio in G for flute, violin and continuo ....*Bach*

Seats bookable : 8/6, 7/-, 5/6, 4/-. Unreserved : 2/6.

THE PALACE THEATRE, BIDEFORD
Wednesday, 29th June, at 7.30 p.m.
The
AMADEUS STRING QUARTET

Quartet in G major, Op. 77, No. 1...............*Haydn*
Quartet K.458 (The Hunt).....................*Mozart*
Quartet in E flat major, Op. 127................*Beethoven*

Seats bookable : 8/6, 7/-, 5/6, 4/-. Unreserved : 2/6.

THEATRE WORKSHOP
in
MOTHER COURAGE
AND HER CHILDREN
by Bertolt Brecht

Characters

Mother Courage	..	.. JOAN LITTLEWOOD
Kattrin, her daughter	..	.. BARBARA BROWN
Eilif	*her*	.. GERARD DYNEVOR
Swiss Cheese	*sons*	.. ISRAEL PRICE
The Chaplain	..	.. HARRY CORBETT
The Cook	..	.. GEORGE A. COOPER
Yvette	..	.. AVIS BUNNAGE
The Colonel	..	.. HOWARD GOORNEY
Recruiting Sergeant	..	..GEORGE LUSCOMBE
Sergeant Major	..	.. MAXWELL SHAW
Commander in Chief	..	.. JOBY BLANSHARD
Ordnance Officer	..	.. BARRY CLAYTON
Young Soldier	..	PETER BRIDGEMONT
Peasant Woman	..	.. ELLEN ORR

Other Characters played by the company

Produced by JOAN LITTLEWOOD

Pianist : Betty Hudson

The DEVON FESTIVAL of the ARTS

June 20th - July 3rd
1955

BARNSTAPLE BIDEFORD ILFRACOMBE

Mother Courage by Bertolt Brecht, 1955
The Devon Festival of Arts had the privilege of the first English
production of the Brecht play. Joan Littlewood played the leading role.

The Midwife by Julya Hay, Translated by A L Lloyd, 1955

The Legend of Pepito by Ted Allen, 1955

The Sheepwell (Fuente Ovejuna) by Lope de Vega, Adapted by Ewan MacColl, 1955

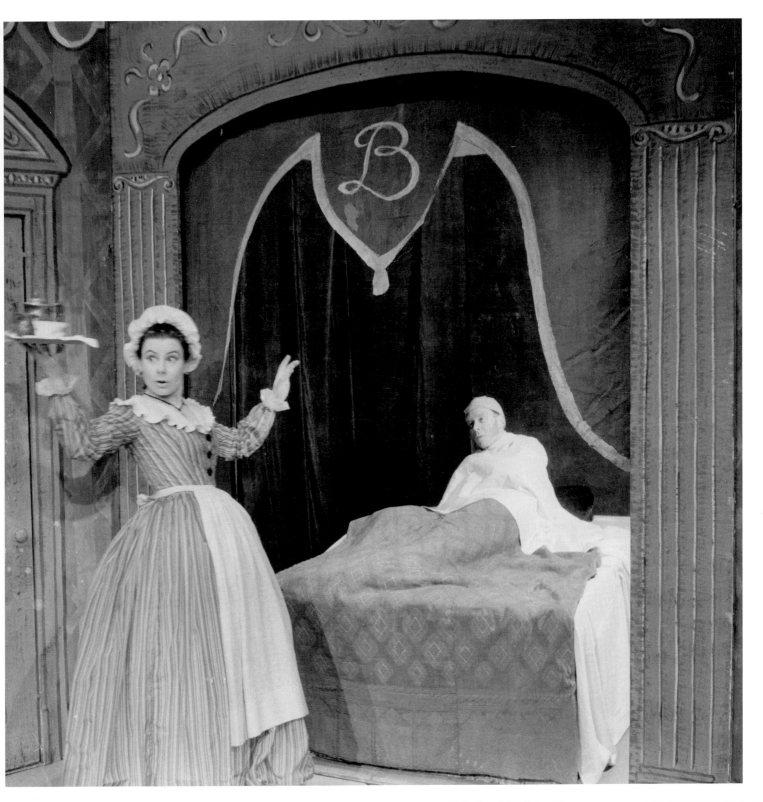

An Italian Straw Hat by Eugene Labiche and Marc Michel,
Translated by Theodore Hoffman, Music by Andre Cadou, 1955

The Big Rock Candy Mountain by Alan Lomax, 1955

1956

Edward II by Christopher Marlowe, 1956
Peter Smallwood gave the most moving performance as Edward in another
outstanding Elizabethan production, and John Bury created an evocative set of
a tilted stage covered with the map of England and his usual magical lighting.

The Quare Fellow by Brendan Behan, 1956
Brendan Behan hits town and the place is never the same again.
An anti-hanging play. Capital punishment was not abolished in
Britain until 1965. The play was at times very funny and then very
disturbing and gave us an insight into the horrors of the system.

Captain Brassbound's Conversion by George Bernard Shaw, 1956
The winter season '56–'57 was directed by John Bury, starting with
Shaw, who had become part of the Workshop's staple diet.

1957

The Playboy of the Western World by John Millington Synge, 1957

The Duchess of Malfy by John Webster, 1957

The School for Wives from Molière's *L'École des Femmes*, Adapted by Miles Malleson, 1957

You Won't Always Be On Top by Henry Chapman, 1957

Joan starts the winter '57 season with an unusual piece. Out goes the stylistic production and in comes naturalism, and the company is off to a local building site to be instructed in the art of brick-laying. John Bury transforms the stage into a three-storey building under construction, plus a cement mixer that works to produce the mortar for the brickies.

And the Wind Blew by Edgard da Rocha Miranda, 1957
A contemporary play set in a small village in Brazil.

1958

Celestina by Fernando de Rojas, Translated by James Mabbe, 1958

Man, Beast and Virtue by Luigi Pirandello, Translated by Edward Eager, 1958
This production was directed by Francis Jamnik from the National Theatre of Slovenia

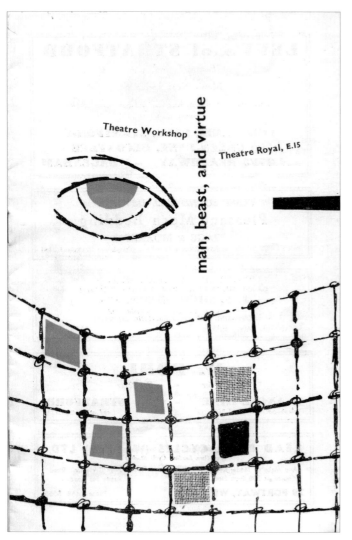

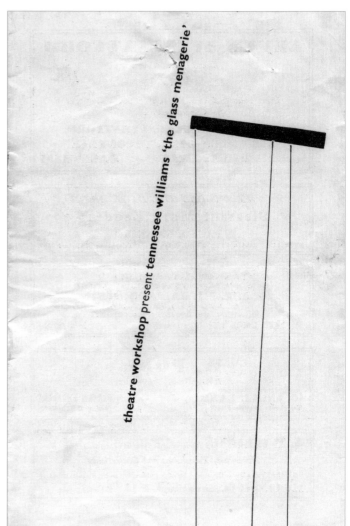

The Glass Menagerie by Tennessee Williams, 1958
Clifford Williams, who had worked with the Workshop in its pre-Stratford days, directed.
Joan Littlewood made one of her periodic appearances on stage as Amanda Wingfield.

Man of Destiny by George Bernard Shaw, 1958 (produced with *Love and Letters*)
This evening of the George Bernard Shaw and Ellen Terry letters
was directed by John Bury, who also designed the set and lighting.

The Respectable Prostitute by Jean-Paul Sartre, Translated by Kitty Black, 1958
The Respectable Prostitute was played by Yootha Joyce; she was magnificent
in the part. The Workshop considered it to be her greatest role. Later she
was in the television series *George and Mildred*.

Unto Such Glory by Paul Green, 1958

A Taste of Honey by Shelagh Delaney, 1958
Received in the post from a 19 year-old from Manchester, this play was to change the fortunes of both Theatre
Workshop and the Theatre Royal. It was given a seminal stage design by John Bury, and the John Wallbank trio in
a stage box completed the magic. It started off as X-certificate and has ended up as schools' certificate.

Theatre Workshop present

Unto Such Glory

by **Paul Green**

The Respectable Prostitute

by **Jean-Paul Sartre**

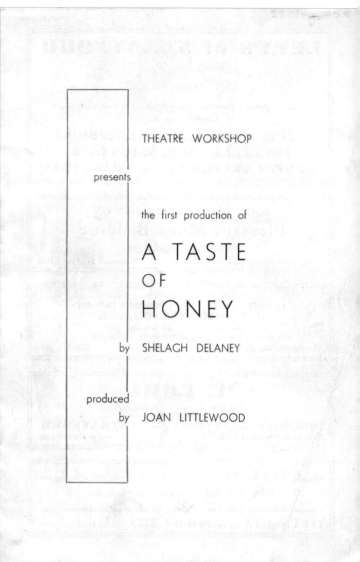

THEATRE WORKSHOP

presents

the first production of

A TASTE
OF
HONEY

by SHELAGH DELANEY

produced

by JOAN LITTLEWOOD

Theatre Royal
Stratford e.15

theatre workshop
presents

produced by
Joan Littlewood

Brendan Behan's

the OsTaGE

The Hostage by Brendan Behan, 1958
It was reported early in rehearsals that the IRA, furious at Brendan for
making fun of them, would attend the first night to 'get him'. As one
review mentioned, 'If the IRA were in attendance with guns, they would
not be able to shoot straight for laughing.' Brendan commented: 'The
big bomb has made me scared of all the little ones.' Behan was back.

A Christmas Carol by Charles Dickens, Adapted by Joan Littlewood, 1958

1959

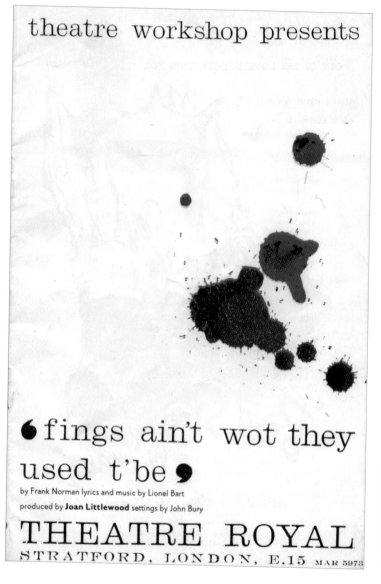

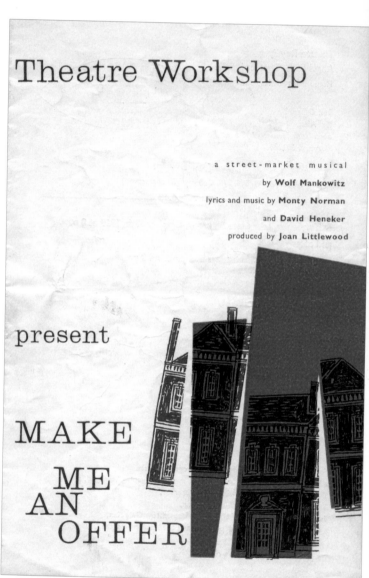

Fings Ain't Wot They Used T'Be by Frank Norman and Lionel Bart, 1959
Soho came to Stratford with songs by Lionel Bart, and low life became the high life of success.

Make Me an Offer by Wolf Mankowitz, 1959

1960

Every Man in His Humour by Ben Jonson, 1960
After the street life of London in the Fifties, the Workshop returned to the
Elizabethan streets in the company of 'O Rare Ben'. This production went to the
Paris Festival and Bob Grant won the Best Actor award for his portrayal of 'Kitely'.

Sparrers Can't Sing by Stephen Lewis, 1960
A day in the life... High rise blocks going up and old communities being destroyed to make way for them.
Stephen Lewis used the concerns of local Stepney people, their dramas and their laughter, and they
appreciated the gesture. The script, reworked, was to be made into a film directed by Joan Littlewood.

OH WHAT A LOVELY WAR, 1963

In the February of 1962 Gerry Raffles heard a BBC radio programme on the history of the Western Front during the First World War. The story was told from the point of view of the ordinary soldier in the trenches; it was interspersed with the popular songs of the time. The programme had been written and produced by Charles Chilton and the songs made such an impact on Gerry that he became certain they could form the basis of a theatrical presentation.

Charles had lost his father in that war, and much later in his life he had gone to the battlefields of Arras to photograph his father's grave. He was shocked to find so many cemeteries in that area. After much searching he failed to find the resting place of his father. But on a wall of the Memorial Arch his name was inscribed along with the names of '35,942 officers and men of the Forces of the British Empire who fell in the Battle of Arras and who have no known graves'.

Charles wrote in the programme of the original production of *Oh What a Lovely War* in March 1963: 'What could have possibly happened to a man that rendered his burial impossible? What horror could have taken place that rendered the burial of 35,942 men impossible and all in one relatively small area? The search for the answer to this question has finally led to this production, in the sincere hope that such an epitaph will never have to be written upon any man's memorial again.'

This was a pivotal time in the history of the First World War. The fifty-year period of secrecy had elapsed and the documents pertaining to the war began to come into the public domain. For the first time since the end of those hostilities, uncomfortable questions about the strategies employed by the British Government and the commanding officers of 1914 could be discussed. Books were beginning to appear, such as the marvellous overall picture of events created by Barbara Tuchman in her *August 1914* (also known as *The Guns of August*).

THEATRE ROYAL E15

a musical entertainment based on an idea of Charles Chilton

designed by John Bury

'OH WHAT A LOVELY WAR'

THEATRE ROYAL

Angel Lane, Stratford, E.15.   Maryland 5973/4
House and Box Office Manager: Alexander Gray
Prices Stalls 15/-, 12/6, 8/6, 6/6
Dress Circle 12/6, 8/6, 6/6 : Upper Circle 3/6 : Gallery 2/-
Box Office open from 10 a.m.

THEATRE WORKSHOP

presents

Oh What a Lovely War

By THEATRE WORKSHOP, CHARLES CHILTON
and the Members of the Cast
(Military Adviser : RAYMOND FLETCHER)

on the basis of factual data in official records, war memoirs,
personal recollections and commentaries including those of :—

The Imperial War Museum	Engelbrecht and Hanighen
Kaiser Wilhelm II	Siegfried Sassoon
General Erich Ludendorff	Sir Philip Gibbs
Field Marshal Graf von Schlieffen	Edmund Blunden
Marshal Joffre	Leon Wolff
Field Marshal Earl Haig	Captain Liddell Hart
Field Marshal Sir John French	Barbara Tuchman
General Sir Henry Wilson	Herman Kahn
Rt. Hon. David Lloyd George	The Times
Philip Noel-Baker	The Daily Express
Alan Clark	

We are especially indebted for personal help to :—
Sgt. Dearsley (Royal Fusiliers)
Dorothy Woodman
Bert Sweet (ex-Gunner, 186 R.F.A., Deptford Gun Brigade) and
    many other ex-members of the armies of both sides in the
    1914-18 war
And above all, to the unknown British soldier-composers of the
    Western Front

First Public Performance Tuesday, March 19th, 1963

So a nucleus of the Workshop company was brought together to
start work on the project. The inspiration was provided by Charles
Chilton's script. Study and absorption of a multitude of facts and the
subsequent improvisation of the salient moments of the War began.
The sources for the material were widespread, as can be seen from the
credits list in the original programme.

The set and lighting were to be designed as usual by the Workshop's
long-serving and brilliant designer John Bury (opposite).

In her book *Joan Littlewood*, Nadine Holdsworth sums up perfectly the rehearsal and production process of *Oh What a Lovely War*:

> In this one production, she successfully combined all the theatrical elements she had previously experimented with from her early days [...] The traditions of popular entertainment – the seaside pierrot show, music-hall, comic turns – sat alongside huge projected slides of recruiting posters and photographic evidence of trench life and war casualties, whilst a 'ticker tape' newspanel flashed contextual information, official death tolls and statistics of battles fought, won and lost. These living newspaper techniques functioned in dynamic interplay with multi-faceted live action: a Master of Ceremonies' jocular interjections and actors performing satirical sketches, vaudevillian acts and realistic scenes of trench life. The acting styles were drawn from agit-prop, music-hall, expressionist and naturalistic traditions and demanded great flexibility from the actors [...] (pp 81–2)

To that list I would add the influence of European innovators that had always guided the Workshop: Eisenstein, Meyerhold, Piscator and Brecht; the Commedia dell'Arte, the Théâtre National Populaire and our own Charlie Chaplin.

It was a production that would change our perspective, not only on the First World War and its leaders, but on the whole of English theatrical presentation.

Una Collins designed the costumes for the production. Her drawings, and the photographs by Romano Cagnoni, appear on the following pages.

'We Don't Want to Lose You' FANNY CARBY

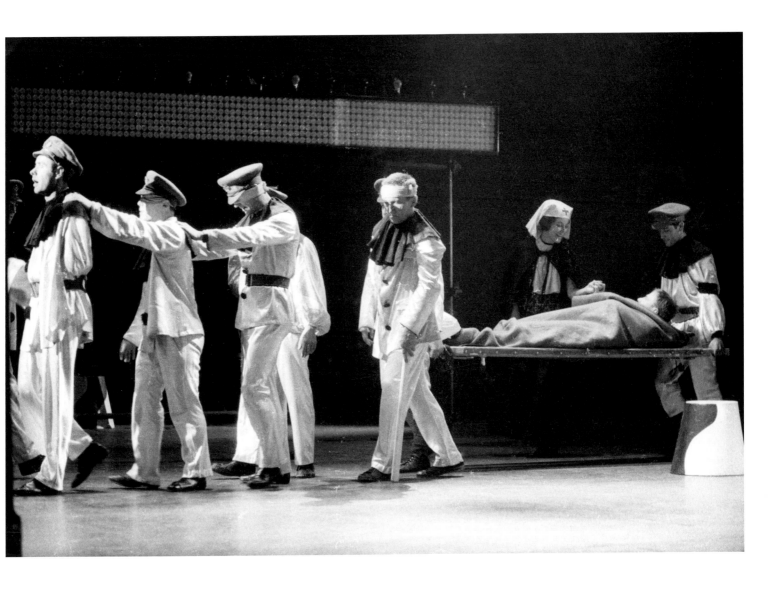

Oh What a Lovely War played in New York in 1964, and this was my last production for Theatre Workshop. Their journey continued, but that task is for another writer. My association with the company and the Theatre Royal continues today in my role as the theatre's archivist.

BEHIND THE SCENES

Over the years the Archive at the Theatre Royal has acquired many
official and personal photographs of the Company and its members.
Many of these are reproduced over the following pages.

New Brighton, 1950: Harry H Corbett and Avis Bunnage
Members of Chorlton Repertory Company, Manchester,
prior to joining Theatre Workshop

Tour of Finland, 1951
Ewan MacColl, Joan Littlewood, John Bury (back row)
Kristin Lind, Doreen Warburton, Rosalie Williams, Harry Greene, Peter Dix (front row)

Barbara Brown and
Peter Bridgemont, 1950s

Theatre Royal Stratford, 1950s
Jo Benson working the lighting board

Theatre Royal Wardrobe, 1955
Jo Wilkinson fitting Avis Bunnage for her costume in *An Italian Straw Hat*

Devon Arts Festival, Barnstaple, 1955
Avis Bunnage, Harry H Corbett, George Luscombe, Betty Hudson (pianist),
Howard Goorney, Barry Clayton, Gerard Dynevor, Israel Price

The Good Soldier Schweik, 1955
John Bury testing the revolve at Theatre Royal Stratford East

Scandinavian tour, January/February 1956
Joan Littlewood and the Company with their hosts

The Good Soldier Schweik, 1956
Gerard Dynevor and Shirley Teague, Sarah Bernhardt Theatre, Paris

The Good Soldier Schweik, 1956
Joan gives notes to the company in the foyer, Sarah Bernhardt Theatre, Paris

You Won't Always Be On Top, October 1957
Dressed for the occasion: summoned to court by the Lord Chamberlain
for 'improvising' on stage without permission. Gerry Raffles,
Joan Littlewood, Richard Harris, Henry Chapman, John Bury

The Wardrobe, 1958
Olive McFarland pressing her costume before a
performance, Theatre Royal Stratford East, 1958

Café L'Ange, Angel Lane, 1958
Murray Melvin, Yootha Joyce, Charles Wood (stage manager
at the time, later a playwright), Una Collins (designer)
Bert Scagnelli, owner

Sarah Bernhardt Theatre, Paris, 1959
Yootha Joyce points to *The Hostage*

Dressing room, Wyndhams Theatre, February 1959: *A Taste of Honey*
Nigel Davenport, Clifton Jones, Murray Melvin, Shelagh Delaney

Sparrers Can't Sing, Copenhagen, 1960

Harry H Corbett, Barbara Ferris, Fanny Carby, Maurice Good

SAVING THE BUILDING

In the late Sixties the local authorities started work on the regeneration of the area around the Theatre Royal. Plans for development included the demolition of the theatre. Gerry Raffles (above) had other ideas. He initiated and obtained a Grade II preservation order on the theatre, which saved the building and secured the future of the Theatre Royal for generations yet to come.

Sadly his early death, aged 51 in 1975, robbed him of the knowledge that the preservation order he obtained has now been increased to Grade II*; that our present local authority of Newham has designated the area the Cultural Quarter of Stratford; that the policy of community theatre, the educational programmes started when the company first arrived at Stratford plus the training programmes for young people in all aspects of theatre, were and are continued by today's administration. It is his and the company's greatest memorial.

'I HAVE BUILT MY LIFE ON THE ROCK OF CHANGE'

Joan Littlewood